Published in 2013 by The Rosen Publishing Group, Inc.
29 East 21st Street, New York, NY 10010

Photo Credits: **KEY** tl=top left; tc=top center; tr=top right; cl=center left; c=center; cr=center right; bl=bottom left; bc=bottom center; br=bottom right; bg=background

CBT = Corbis; DT = Dreamstime; GI = Getty Images; iS = istockphoto.com; N = NASA; SH = Shutterstock; TF = Topfoto

front cover bg SH; bl GI; **back cover** tl GI; bc iS; **1**c SH; **2–3**bg SH; **4–5**bg CBT; **6**cl iS; bl SH; **8**tr SH; **9**c CBT; **10**br, tr SH; bl, tl TF; **10–11**bg SH; **11**bl, br, tl TF; **12**cl, cr SH; **13**c CBT; cl, cr SH; tr TF; **14**bl; **14**tr iS; **16**br, cr, tr N; **17**tr iS; cl SH; **18**cl DT; **18–19**bg CBT; **19**br, cl CBT; tr SH; **20**bl iS; c TF; **20–21**c **20–21**bg iS; **21**bl, br, c, cr CBT; tc, tl iS; **22**tr SH; **22–23**bc iS; **23**br, c iS; **24**cl iS; tr TF; **24–25**bc GI; **25**tl iS; tr SH; **26**bl iS; **26–27**tc SH; **27**br, c, tr SH; **28**tl iS; **28–29**cr N; **31**bc iS; **32**bg iS

All illustrations copyright Weldon Owen Pty Ltd. Andrew Davies

Weldon Owen Pty Ltd
Managing Director: Kay Scarlett
Creative Director: Sue Burk
Publisher: Helen Bateman
Senior Vice President, International Sales: Stuart Laurence
Vice President Sales North America: Ellen Towell
Administration Manager, International Sales: Kristine Ravn

Library of Congress Cataloging-in-Publication Data

Einspruch, Andrew.
 Overpopulation / by Andrew Einspruch. — 1st ed.
     p. cm. — (Discovery education: The environment)
 Includes index.
 ISBN 978-1-4488-7890-1 (library binding) — ISBN 978-1-4488-7978-6 (pbk.) — ISBN 978-1-4488-7984-7 (6-pack)
 1. Overpopulation—Juvenile literature. 2. Population—Juvenile literature. 3. Population—Environmental aspects—Juvenile literature. I. Title.
 HB883.E46 2013
 363.9′1—dc23
                               2011048214

Manufactured in the United States of America

CPSIA Compliance Information: Batch #SW12PK: For Further Information contact Rosen Publishing, New York, New York at 1-800-237-9932

Discovery EDUCATION

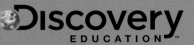

THE ENVIRONMENT

OVERPOPULATION

ANDREW EINSPRUCH

PowerKiDS press

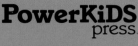

New York

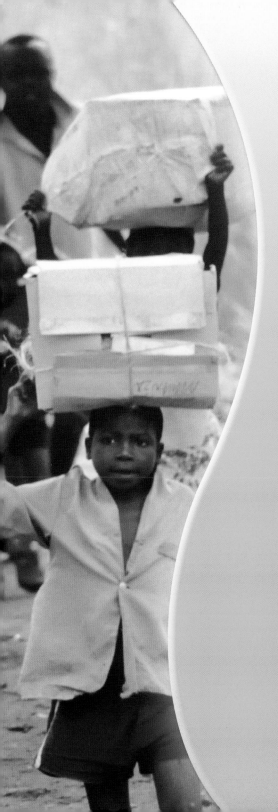

Contents

Population Density

Population density describes how closely packed together people are in a place. If you compare cities to country towns, there are more people per square mile (km) in a city than in the country. So cities have a higher population density than country towns. Nations are similar. Some nations have large numbers of people in a small space, while others have much more space than people.

Population density is one way to compare the different countries on Earth. It affects how people in those countries live, and the different opportunities and problems they face.

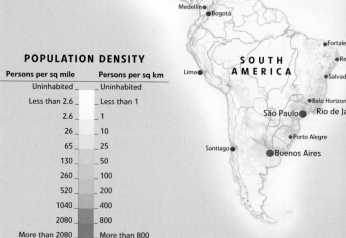

Skyscrapers in Manhattan, part of New York City

Mongolian yurts at Kanas Lake, Xinjiang, northwest China

From country to city
In the last few hundred years, millions of people have moved to the cities. These days, people are more likely to live crammed into places like Manhattan than in sparse regions like Xinjiang in northwest China and Mongolia.

POPULATION DENSITY

Persons per sq mile	Persons per sq km
Uninhabited	Uninhabited
Less than 2.6	Less than 1
2.6	1
26	10
65	25
130	50
260	100
520	200
1040	400
2080	800
More than 2080	More than 800

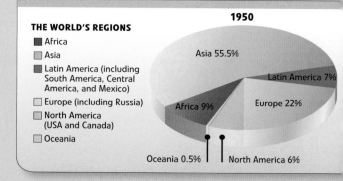

THE WORLD'S REGIONS
- Africa
- Asia
- Latin America (including South America, Central America, and Mexico)
- Europe (including Russia)
- North America (USA and Canada)
- Oceania

1950

Asia 55.5%

Latin America 7%

Africa 9%

Europe 22%

Oceania 0.5%

North America 6%

The three places with the highest population density are Macau, Monaco, and Hong Kong. The three with the lowest density are Greenland, Svalbard, and the Falkland Islands.

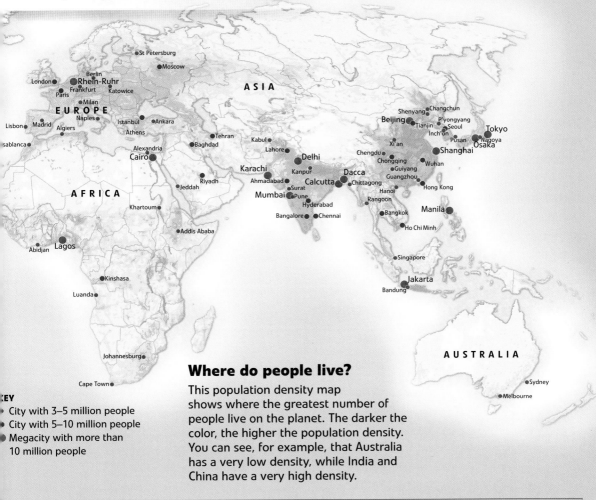

Where do people live?

This population density map shows where the greatest number of people live on the planet. The darker the color, the higher the population density. You can see, for example, that Australia has a very low density, while India and China have a very high density.

KEY
- City with 3–5 million people
- City with 5–10 million people
- Megacity with more than 10 million people

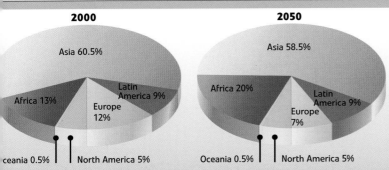

2000
- Asia 60.5%
- Africa 13%
- Europe 12%
- Latin America 9%
- Oceania 0.5%
- North America 5%

2050
- Asia 58.5%
- Africa 20%
- Europe 7%
- Latin America 9%
- Oceania 0.5%
- North America 5%

WHERE IN THE WORLD?

Asia is expected to maintain its share of the world's population at about 60 percent. The big shifts are Europe and Africa. In 1950, Europe had twice as many people as Africa had. By 2000, Africa had more, and is expected to have three times the population of Europe by 2050.

Exploding Population

The biggest single change on Earth in the past 250 years is the explosion in the human population. We have taken over the planet, pushing all other species aside. More and more people make more and more demands on the planet. Some people believe that the number of humans cannot keep growing at this rapid rate if we are to survive.

Population growth is both an opportunity and a problem. A greater number of people means more chances for innovation and prosperity. However, it also means there are more people who need food, water, shelter, and health care.

That's Amazing!

About 10,000 years ago, there were only 5–10 million humans. Around AD 1, the population leveled out at 300 million. Then it exploded around 1750 with the Industrial Revolution.

China's population

China has more people than any other country on Earth. In fact, one out of every five people on the planet lives there. It is estimated that China will see its population grow to more than 1.4 billion by 2050, up from just 545 million in 1950.

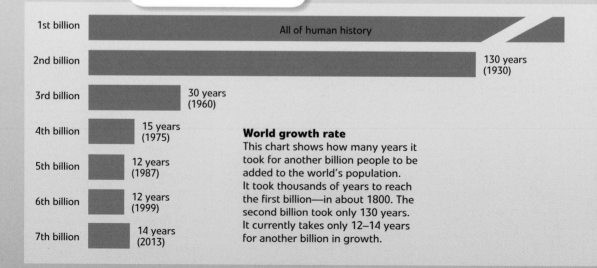

1st billion	All of human history
2nd billion	130 years (1930)
3rd billion	30 years (1960)
4th billion	15 years (1975)
5th billion	12 years (1987)
6th billion	12 years (1999)
7th billion	14 years (2013)

World growth rate

This chart shows how many years it took for another billion people to be added to the world's population. It took thousands of years to reach the first billion—in about 1800. The second billion took only 130 years. It currently takes only 12–14 years for another billion in growth.

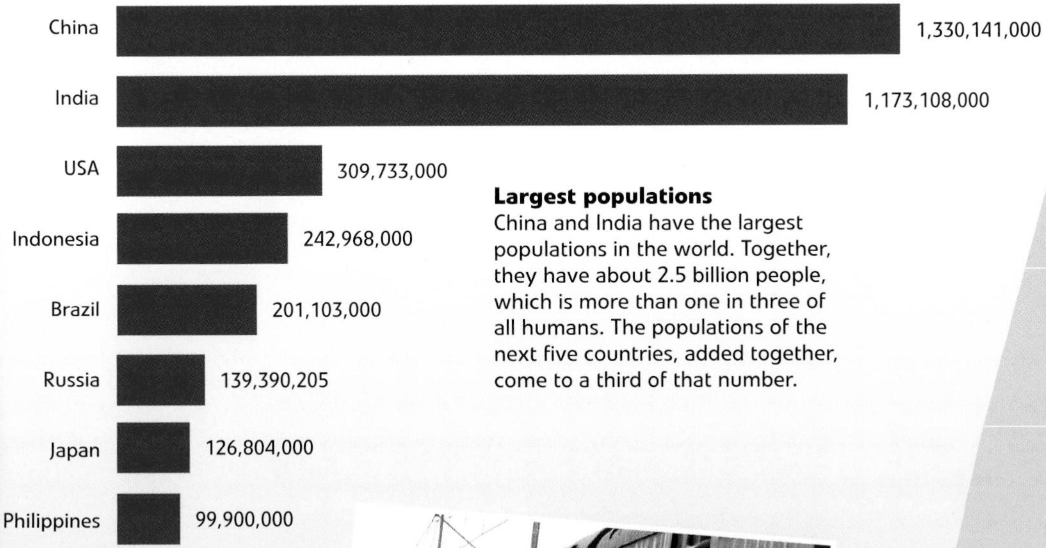

China — 1,330,141,000

India — 1,173,108,000

USA — 309,733,000

Indonesia — 242,968,000

Brazil — 201,103,000

Russia — 139,390,205

Japan — 126,804,000

Philippines — 99,900,000

Largest populations

China and India have the largest populations in the world. Together, they have about 2.5 billion people, which is more than one in three of all humans. The populations of the next five countries, added together, come to a third of that number.

India's population

India's population crossed the 1 billion mark in 2000 and is growing faster than China's. If current trends continue, it will take the number one spot by 2030, with 1.46 billion people to China's 1.39 billion people.

How high can it go?

This chart shows how fast populations have grown. It is impossible to know exactly what will happen in the future, but current growth rates have the world's population doubling every 60 years or so. That would mean 13 billion people by 2067.

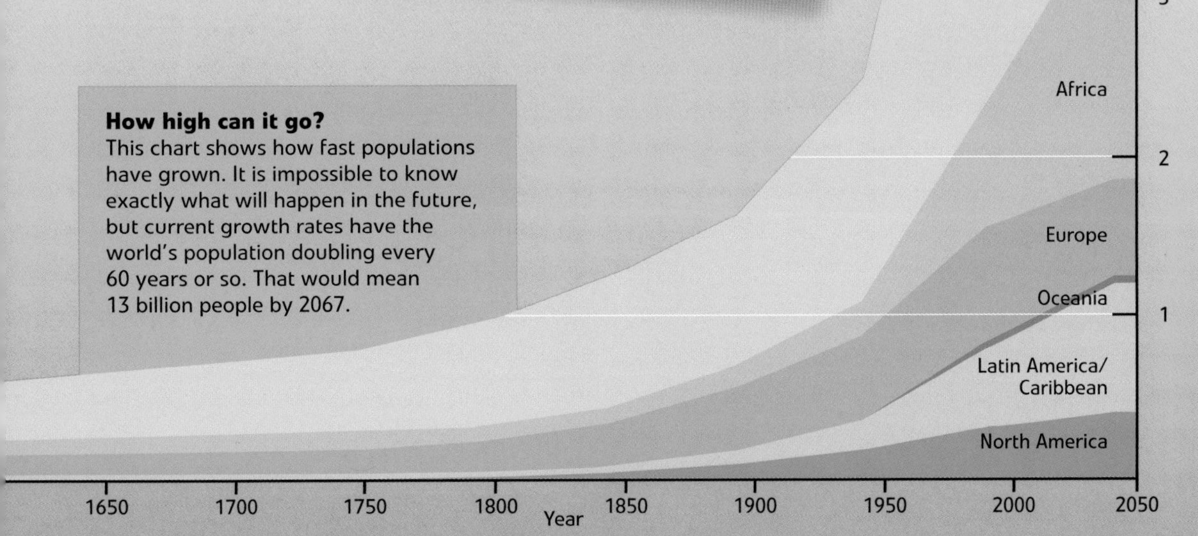

Total world population (billions)

Asia

Africa

Europe

Oceania

Latin America/ Caribbean

North America

8

7

6

5

4

3

2

1

1650   1700   1750   1800   1850   1900   1950   2000   2050

Year

CASE STUDY: CHINA
Country Life

My name is Hua Shan
I live in Pengzhou, which is in Sichuan, China, where my family has a farm. Here I am walking to school past the paddies that my family has farmed for many generations. We grow mainly rice.

Fishing
My grandfather on my mother's side has always loved fishing. Here he has caught something for dinner. He sometimes takes me with him on his boat.

Meet my little brother
My little brother is too young for school, but not too young to help out. Hua Ming has just fed our chickens, which was my job when I was his age.

Downtime
My grandfather on my father's side is relaxing with two of his friends. He still helps out with the farming when it gets busy, but he has turned most of the work over to my father.

Farming
Our neighbors also farm. They specialize in growing radishes. Here they are washing some freshly dug white radishes, getting them ready for market.

Going to market
My mother uses a bicycle cart to transport some of our farm's goods to market. The market is fairly close, so it is not too hard for her to take the produce there.

Ox and plow
This is my favorite uncle, Hua Tian, plowing a field with a plow pulled by a water buffalo. He is preparing the field, getting it ready to sow seed for a new season of crops.

Why Does Population Grow?

The population of the world is growing for a number of reasons. At one level, it is simple mathematics. If you have two people, and they have more than two children, then you end up with more people.

But it is not quite that simple. Modern improvements to the way we live—such as clean water, more food, and better medicine—have meant that fewer children die all around the world. Also, people are living longer. This means that the number of people on the planet continues to increase.

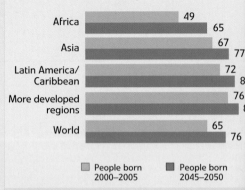

Africa	49	
	65	
Asia	67	
	77	
Latin America/ Caribbean	72	
	8	
More developed regions	76	
	8	
World	65	
	76	

■ People born 2000–2005   ■ People born 2045–2050

Life expectancy
Life expectancy is how many years people, on average, are expected to live from the time they are born. Across the world, people are expected to live much longer lives in the decades to come.

Babies survive
More babies are living to become adults. Health programs have focused on preventing or treating common illnesses that babies can die from, such as diarrhea, malaria, and pneumonia.

Decline in birthrate
The birthrate is how many children are born for every 1,000 women of childbearing age. Throughout the world, this rate has been going down for decades. But even so, the total number of people keeps growing because there are more and more women.

KEY
■ Women age 15–49
— Average number of children per woman

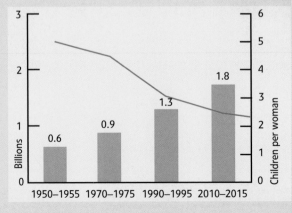

Billions: 0.6 | 0.9 | 1.3 | 1.8

1950–1955 1970–1975 1990–1995 2010–2015

Children per woman

Older people
On average, the world's population is getting older. For example, in Japan, more than 20 percent of the people are aged over 65, and that is expected to reach 40 percent by about 2055.

INDUSTRIAL REVOLUTION

From around 1750, at the beginning of the Industrial Revolution, sanitation and health care both started to improve. This meant that fewer children and young people died. Transportation and communication also improved. If crops failed in one place, people found out about it, and food could be shipped to that area so the people would not starve.

A factory in London, England, around 1840

Clean water
A key to improved human health and longevity is clean water. Contaminated water can carry bacteria, viruses, and protozoa that cause illnesses such as cholera, botulism, and dysentery. All of these illnesses can be fatal.

Medical advances
Improved medical treatment and health care means that things that used to kill people no longer do. Infections and diseases that used to wipe out thousands are routinely treated by medicines that are common and easy to get.

Large-scale farming
Large-scale farming means that it takes fewer people to produce more and more food. While some people question the quality and safety of the food grown this way, the fact is that food is more plentiful and cheaper than ever before.

Shrinking, Swelling, Surging

Population numbers do not change in the same way across the planet. Some countries' populations are booming, others are holding steady, and some are actually getting smaller. This may be due to the birthrate, but not always. A country with a low birthrate may receive immigrants, who increase numbers. Longevity plays an important role. So do cultural factors, which can affect whether people want big or small families.

Sometimes, governments actively encourage smaller or larger families. And sadly, events such as war, famine, and epidemics can strongly affect a country's population.

Liberia
One of the fastest growing nations is the Republic of Liberia on the west coast of Africa. It was colonized by freed American slaves in the 1820s, and is considered one of the poorest countries on Earth. Its annual population growth rate is about 3.7 percent.

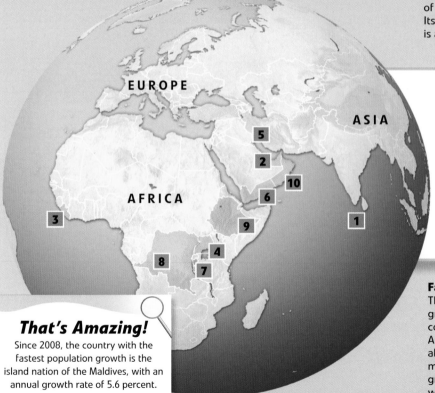

EUROPE

ASIA

AFRICA

FASTEST GROWING COUNTRIES

1	Maldives	5.6%
2	United Arab Emirates	3.8%
3	Liberia	3.7%
4	Uganda	3.6%
5	Kuwait	3.6%
6	Yemen	3.5%
7	Burundi	3.4%
8	Democratic Republic of Congo	3.2%
9	Ethiopia	3.2%
10	Oman	3.19%

Fastest growing countries
The countries with the fastest growing populations in the world come mainly from two regions: Africa and the Middle East. They all have an annual growth rate of more than 3 percent. A 3.5 percent growth rate means the population will double in about 20 years.

That's Amazing!
Since 2008, the country with the fastest population growth is the island nation of the Maldives, with an annual growth rate of 5.6 percent.

rom shrinking to surging

nese dolls give a sense of the relative population growth
tes of selected countries. The bigger the doll, the faster the
opulation growth. So, for example, even though China has a
uge population, its growth is modest, so its doll is small.

United States
The United States
has shown slow and
steady population
growth for decades.

Russia
Russia's population
is shrinking because
of a big drop in
the birthrate.

China
China has a fairly
low birthrate, but
the population
continues to grow.

Australia
Australia accepts
a regular number
of immigrants,
who help boost
its population.

Shrinking or steady

Brazil
The population
is rising due to
improvements
in health and a
steady birthrate.

Ireland
Ireland's cities
have swollen
because many
migrant workers
from Europe
moved there.

India
India's population is
huge and growing,
in part due to better
health care and a
high birthrate.

Swelling

Saudi Arabia
The population is
surging because of
high immigration,
a high birthrate, and
improved longevity.

Liberia
The population of
Liberia is exploding
because the country
has an extremely
high birthrate.

Surging

Biggest Cities

I t is in the cities of the world where population growth is really happening. It used to be that cities grew huge only in developed countries such as the USA and the UK. Today, big cities are dotted around the globe, with some of the biggest being found in the developing countries of Asia.

These cities are so huge they are called megacities, with much larger populations than entire countries. For example, if Tokyo were a country, it would have the 34th highest population in the world, ahead of countries such as Canada, Algeria, and Afghanistan.

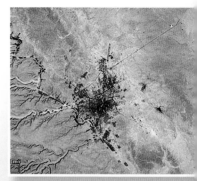

Riyadh in 1972

Rank	Megacity	Country	Continent	Population
1	Tokyo	Japan	Asia	36,670,000
2	Delhi	India	Asia	22,160,000
3	São Paulo	Brazil	South America	20,260,000
4	Mumbai	India	Asia	20,040,000
5	Mexico City	Mexico	North America	19,460,000
6	New York City	USA	North America	19,430,000
7	Shanghai	China	Asia	16,580,000
8	Calcutta	India	Asia	15,550,000
9	Dhaka	Bangladesh	Asia	14,650,000
10	Karachi	Pakistan	Asia	13,120,000
11	Buenos Aires	Argentina	South America	13,070,000
12	Los Angeles	USA	North America	12,760,000
13	Beijing	China	Asia	12,390,000
14	Rio de Janeiro	Brazil	South America	11,950,000
15	Manila	Philippines	Asia	11,630,000
16	Osaka	Japan	Asia	11,340,000

Riyadh in 1990

Riyadh in 2000

World's top megacities
Asia dominates the list of the world's top megacities, with 10 million people or more. These figures include the cities' surrounding areas. Of the top 16, ten are in Asian countries, mostly in developing Asian countries. Between them, China and India alone have five of these megacities.

Boom city Riyadh
Money from oil dollars fueled a huge building boom in Riyadh, Saudi Arabia's capital, as these aerial photos show. The city's population grew from 30,000 in 1972 to 500,000 in 2000.

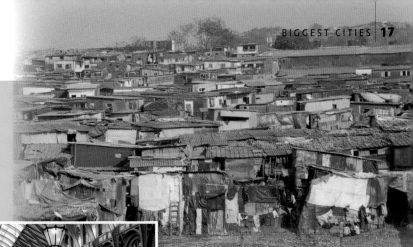

Rich and poor

Cities display the very best and very worst of humanity. The intense concentration of people can create a vibrant culture. But it can also bring poverty and squalor.

Mumbai slums

The second largest slum in the world, Dharavi, is in the middle of Mumbai, India. It has 1 million inhabitants, with 18,000 people crammed into each 1 acre (0.4 ha).

London culture

London, England, is known for its rich culture. It has symphony orchestras and shopping, museums and musicals, food from around the world, and a busy nightlife.

Most populous cities

In 1950, the city with the largest population was New York City, with 12 million inhabitants. Tokyo, now the most populous city, will have triple that number of residents by 2015. Most of the world's big cities are in the developing world now.

1950

London	Tokyo	New York City
8 million	11 million	12 million

2000

New York City	Mexico City	Tokyo
17 million	18 million	34 million

2015

Mumbai	Delhi	Tokyo
21 million	24 million	37 million

My name is Satomi Takahashi
I live in Tokyo, Japan—the city with more people than any other city in the world. It is a very crowded place to live, and one of the world's most expensive. My parents and I live together in a small apartment.

APARTMENT LIVING

Our apartment home uses space very efficiently. For example, we sleep on bedrolls, which are put away during the day so the rooms can be used for other purposes. Our apartment is a good size for a couple with one child (me!).

KEY

1 Entrance hall
2 Bathroom and toilet
3 Shower and bath
4 Parents' bedroom at night; formal living room by day
5 Living room
6 Kitchen
7 Bedroom
8 Storage areas

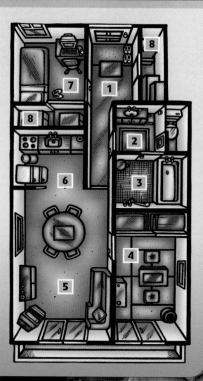

Urban sprawl

It is hard to imagine that Tokyo was once a small fishing village. Today, there is urban sprawl as far as you can see. Tokyo was badly damaged twice in the last century, once by earthquake and once by war, and it was fully rebuilt.

Public swimming pool

When summer comes, people go to swimming pools like this one to cool down in the heat. You just have to share the pool with up to 13,000 others. Sometimes you cannot see the water for all of the people.

Commuters

My father and I commute by train every day. The trains are incredibly crowded and it is common for people to commute for four hours every day to get to school or work.

Changing Countries

One way in which a nation's population changes is when people migrate from one country to another. There are many reasons why people do this. Sometimes, it is for a negative reason—people need to leave a bad situation, such as a war or famine. In other instances, the motivation is positive—they go to a country that offers greater opportunities. And sometimes it is personal—people want to move to be with family or to marry a person they have met.

Many reasons to migrate

All around the world, people are on the move from one country to another. Their individual reasons for moving may vary, but overall, people migrate because they are seeking a better life.

NET MIGRATION RATE

- Positive (more entering country than leaving it)
- Stable (same number entering and leaving country)
- Negative (more people leaving country than entering it)
- No data

NORTH AMERICA

SOUTH AMERICA

SEASONAL MIGRANTS

Fruit and vegetable farmers need extra help when it is time for harvesting their crops. In agricultural areas, there is a long history of migrant workers providing this labor. These workers travel from place to place, working the fields, picking different crops as the seasons change.

Migrant farm workers picking bell peppers in California

Mexico
Many Mexicans cross into the United States illegally, looking for work. Some stay for years, in constant fear that they may suddenly be discovered and sent home.

Desertification

Desertification is when habitable land turns into desert. When this occurs, the land cannot grow food anymore and the people must leave for somewhere new.

Uganda

Decades of war and political unrest have created hundreds of thousands of Ugandan refugees, who fled the turbulence of their country.

Tuvalu

Rising sea levels caused by global warming will swamp low-lying islands such as Tuvalu, or make them uninhabitable as increasing soil salinity destroys crops.

EUROPE

ASIA

AFRICA

AUSTRALIA

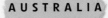

United Arab Emirates (UAE)

Migrant workers make up about 80 percent of the UAE's population. These workers are attracted by job opportunities and salaries, which are higher than in their own countries.

Democratic Republic of Congo

This country, which used to be called Zaire, has a history of war and conflict. This has created a refugee crisis as millions have been forced to flee their homes.

Australia

Australia is a sparsely populated, prosperous country. Thousands of immigrants arrive each year, seeking the many economic opportunities that can be found there.

Kids Matter

One challenge facing all nations, whether their population is growing or not, is providing for the needs of their children. Rapid population growth adds to the challenge. The more children a country has, the more difficult it is to provide everything they need to help them survive and grow into happy members of their society.

There are ways to measure how well a country provides for its children. Factors such as health care, sanitation, the food and water supply, and education reveal whether children have what they need to live and thrive. The number of children who die is also a telling factor.

Clean drinking water
Clean water that is safe to drink is a key to anyone's survival. But children, especially young children, are more vulnerable to diseases carried by unsafe water. In poor countries and in slums, finding clean water can be difficult.

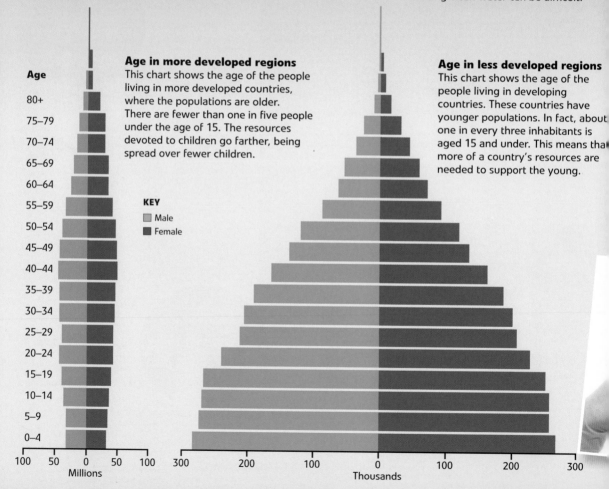

Age in more developed regions
This chart shows the age of the people living in more developed countries, where the populations are older. There are fewer than one in five people under the age of 15. The resources devoted to children go farther, being spread over fewer children.

Age in less developed regions
This chart shows the age of the people living in developing countries. These countries have younger populations. In fact, about one in every three inhabitants is aged 15 and under. This means that more of a country's resources are needed to support the young.

KEY
- Male
- Female

Age

80+
75–79
70–74
65–69
60–64
55–59
50–54
45–49
40–44
35–39
30–34
25–29
20–24
15–19
10–14
5–9
0–4

100 50 0 50 100
Millions

300 200 100 0 100 200 300
Thousands

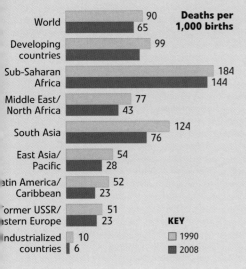

	Deaths per 1,000 births
World	90 / 65
Developing countries	99
Sub-Saharan Africa	184 / 144
Middle East/ North Africa	77 / 43
South Asia	124 / 76
East Asia/ Pacific	54 / 28
Latin America/ Caribbean	52 / 23
Former USSR/ Eastern Europe	51 / 23
Industrialized countries	10 / 6

KEY
☐ 1990
■ 2008

Child mortality

This chart shows mortality, or death, rates for children under five in different regions of the world. Everywhere has improved. The mortality rate has dropped in all regions in recent years. However, it is still highest in developing regions.

Immunization

Immunization has been credited with stopping diseases such as diphtheria, tetanus, and polio, which used to permanently damage or kill thousands of children every year. Public health officials work hard to get vaccines to children around the world.

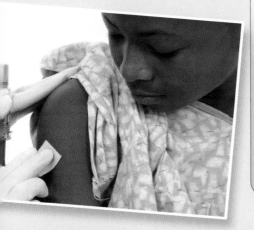

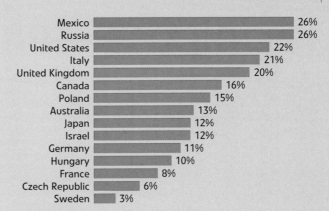

Mexico	26%
Russia	26%
United States	22%
Italy	21%
United Kingdom	20%
Canada	16%
Poland	15%
Australia	13%
Japan	12%
Israel	12%
Germany	11%
Hungary	10%
France	8%
Czech Republic	6%
Sweden	3%

Child poverty

This chart shows the percentage of children living in poverty in certain countries in the 1990s. It shows how even prosperous nations, such as Sweden, could improve the lives of the children living within their borders.

Food

Just like water, food is essential for survival. The sad reality is that many people on Earth do not have enough food, and famine causes the deaths of thousands of children each year.

GETTING AN EDUCATION

Education is crucial to success in life, and all children need it, whether they are rich or poor. A good education opens up opportunities that uneducated people cannot access. It is also important in keeping population numbers under control. Statistics clearly show that educated girls and women have fewer children, no matter where they live in the world.

Students learning to use a computer

Facing Challenges

As populations grow, more demands are placed on social and environmental systems. People want and need a place to live, food to eat, and good health. However, an area that easily supported 100 people and a particular lifestyle for centuries may collapse when the number of people grows to 1,000 or even 10,000. An expanding population can push out and even destroy the very things in a place that once made it possible to survive and prosper there.

The more humans there are on Earth, the more care we need to take of the environment and the natural world, which make life possible.

Hunting
Hunting animals was a way of life for thousands of years. But if too many people need to hunt those animals, and they build their homes where animals once lived, the the number of animals plummets.

Finding homes
Everybody needs somewhere to live. As the number of people on the planet increases, more and more land, which was once used for farming or simply left as habitat for wild animals, is being converted into suburbs and housing.

Collecting water
One feared result of global warming is the increase in El Niño weather events, which cause devastating droughts in places such as Indonesia and parts of Australia. If the rains do not fall, people must bring water from somewhere else—if they can find any.

Health

There is a limit to how much health care any country can provide. There are only so many doctors and health professionals to go around, and health care costs money. The more people there are, the harder it is to provide them all with a high, or even a basic, standard of health care.

Fishing

Like hunting, fishing has sustained people for thousands of years. However, many areas have been overfished. Water pollution and demands on rivers and the sea have also decreased the number of fish available.

Droughts severely affect animal populations, which cannot find food and water either. Lower animal numbers affect the humans around them.

Threats

The big question is, can an ever-growing number of humans survive on the planet? The answer is not clear. Earth has limited resources—in its landmasses, its water sources, and the atmosphere. Ultimately, we humans, as a species, must make do with what is here. Our survival is directly linked to the care that we give to the planet, and to the wisdom with which we use its resources.

If we do not take care of the environment and use Earth's resources in a sustainable way, then the threats to humanity are many.

Agriculture and commercial farming
Technology has helped fewer people grow more food on less land than ever before. But global warming caused by humans is changing weather patterns. This threatens the ability of farmers to grow enough food for a booming world population.

A mass of people
Simple things such as housing, health care, clean water, and sanitation become more difficult to provide as populations expand. There is no guarantee that we will be able to meet the needs, much less the wants, of millions more people.

Industrial pollution

Pollution from industries is a huge ongoing threat to the world. The more things we make to meet our wants and needs, the more pollution and waste we create. Sustainable industries with environmentally responsible practices will help solve this problem.

Deforestation

Vast areas of trees are being cut down every day. However, trees play a critical role in converting carbon dioxide to oxygen for the air we breathe, as well as storing carbon. Deforestation is a direct threat to our survival.

Renewable energy

We need to use renewable sources of energy instead of burning fossil fuels to meet our growing energy needs. Renewable energy, such as wind power and solar power, comes from natural sources that do not run out and do not emit carbon—unlike fossil fuels, such as coal and gas.

About 360,000 people are born each day. And about 155,000 people die each day. The difference is worldwide population growth.

Traditional ways

This Masai family in Kenya still lives in the traditional way. But as populations expand and migrate, especially when people lose or have to leave their traditional lands, it becomes very difficult for them to maintain their cultural heritage and practices.

Find Out More

There are an incredible number of resources available for births, deaths, and population growth and trends. A good place to look first is Wikipedia (www.wikipedia.org). Try searching for "population," "population growth," "census," or "population density" to get started.

You can find information about different countries and their populations by looking at the World Factbook from the Central Intelligence Agency (CIA). Search for "CIA World Factbook" or go to www.cia.gov and find the link on the front page.

There are thousands of other Internet sites with great information. Try typing "population" or "environmental problems" into your favorite search engine.

WORLD POPULATION CLOCK

Search online for "population clock" to find counters that tick over as people are born or die in the world. These counters show the rate of natural increase of the world's population. Natural increase is the number of births minus the number of deaths. The information in the table (right) is the World Population Clock data from the Population Reference Bureau (www.prb.org).

Natural increase per	World	More developed countries	Less developed countries
Year	83,315,475	2,130,380	81,185,094
Month	6,942,956	177,532	6,765,425
Week	1,602,221	40,969	1,561,252
Day	228,262	5,837	222,425
Hour	9,511	243	9,268
Minute	158	4	154
Second	2.6	0.1	2.5

World in lights

This NASA image shows the world as if it were night everywhere. The lights of the populated areas are visible from space, and they show where populations are most dense. The dark areas are where there are few or no people.

Glossary

birthrate (BERTH-rayt)
The number of babies born per 1,000 women of childbearing age.

commuter (kah-MYOO-ter)
Someone who regularly travels from home to work.

culture (KUL-chur)
The customs, art, and behaviors of a particular group of people.

deforestation
(dee-for-uh-STAY-shun)
The large-scale removal of trees.

density (DEN-seh-tee)
The collection or concentration of something in a particular area.

desertification
(dih-zer-tih-fih-KAY-shin)
The gradual change of fertile land into desert.

El Niño (EL NEE-nyoh)
A weather phenomenon that happens in the Pacific Ocean. It combines a rising ocean temperature and a change of winds that shifts where rain falls, causing drought in some areas and floods in others.

global warming
(GLOH-bul WAWRM-ing)
The steady rise in the average temperature of the world, and the associated problems this brings.

growth rate (GROTH RAYT)
The rate, or speed, at which something grows.

habitable (HA-bih-tuh-bul)
Describes a place that is suitable for people to live.

Industrial Revolution
(in-DUS-tree-ul reh-vuh-LOO-shun) A period in history when society changed from being based on agriculture to a society based on industry and manufacturing.

life expectancy
(LYF ik-SPEK-tin-see) The period of time a person is likely to live.

longevity (lon-JEH-vih-tee)
The length of life.

megacities
(MEH-guh sih-tees) An urban area with more than 10 million people.

migrant workers
(MY-grunt WERK-urs) People who move from one country to another for work.

mortality rate
(mor-TAH-lih-tee RAYT)
The number of deaths per year.

NASA (NA-suh) Short for National Aeronautics and Space Administration, this organization controls the US space exploration program.

natural increase
(NA-chuh-rul IN-krees)
The number of births less the number of deaths.

net migration rate
(NET my-GRAY-shun RAYT)
The difference between the number of people entering a country and the number leaving.

poverty (PAH-ver-tee)
The state of having little or no money and few possessions.

refugee (reh-fyoo-JEE)
Someone who leaves their home country for fear of persecution or worry over their safety.

renewable energy
(ree-NOO-uh-bul EH-nur-jee)
Energy taken from natural sources that do not run out, such as solar and wind power.

seasonal migrants
(SEEZ-nul MY-grunts) People who move with the seasons following work opportunities, and not staying in one place permanently.

slum (SLUM) A part of a city characterized by poverty and bad living conditions.

sparse (SPAHRS) Thinly spread; scattered.

sustainable
(suh-STAY-nuh-bel) Able to be kept going.

urban sprawl
(UR-bun SPRAWL) The spread in land occupied by an urban area.

Index

Websites

Due to the changing nature of Internet links, PowerKids Press has developed an online list of websites related to the subject of this book. This site is updated regularly. Please use this link to access the list: www.powerkidslinks.com/disc/over/